CHECK FOR
AUDIO CD IN
FRONT OF BOOK

States & Capitals

Written By:

Kim Mitzo Thompson
Karen Mitzo Hilderbrand

Illustrated By:

Goran Kozjak

Cover Illustration By:

Sandy Haight

Musical Scores By:

Hal Wright

Twin 406 – States & Capitals   (Tape/Book Set) – ISBN# 1-882331-24-9
                                 (CD/Book Set) –   ISBN# 1-57583-296-8

Twin Sisters Productions, Inc. • (800) 248-TWIN • www.twinsisters.com

Table of Contents

My State Flag

Each state has a state flag. Look in an encyclopedia to find out what your state flag looks like. Draw your flag below. Write in the name of your state's capital.

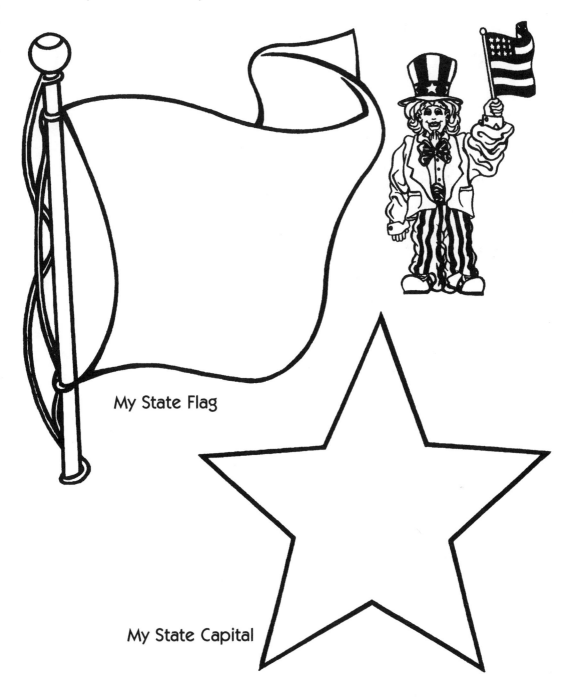

My State Flag

My State Capital

TWIN 406 - States and Capitals

All About My State

My State Flower

My State Tree

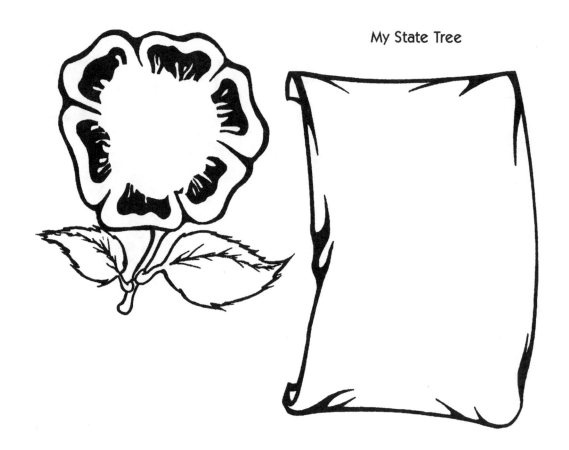

My State Motto

Learning About My State

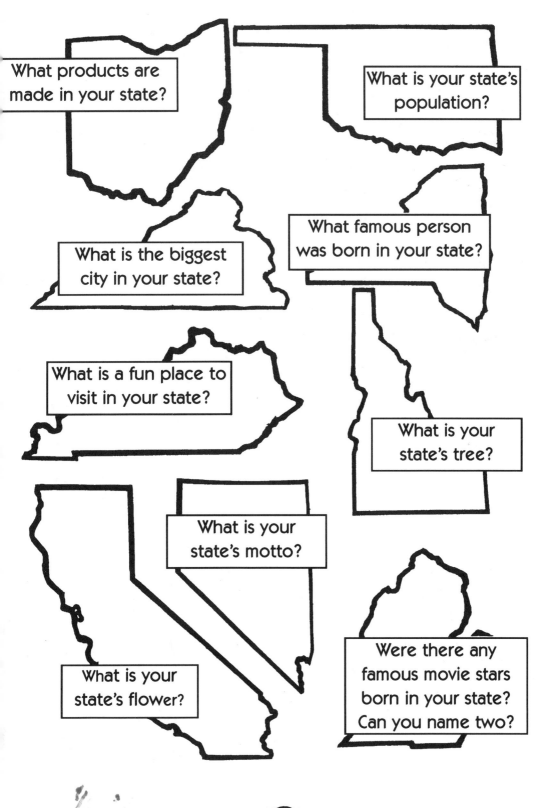

What products are made in your state?

What is your state's population?

What is the biggest city in your state?

What famous person was born in your state?

What is a fun place to visit in your state?

What is your state's tree?

What is your state's motto?

What is your state's flower?

Were there any famous movie stars born in your state? Can you name two?

Improving Our Schools

You have just been elected governor of your state. You are asked to make changes that would improve the schools in your state. What changes would you make? How would you help? What things would you ask the students and teachers to do that would help? Be specific.

TWIN 406 - States and Capitals

President Of The United States

Pick a past president of the United States. Pretend that you are that person and describe what it was like to live in their time. Tell what problems our country was facing at that time. What kind of clothes did people wear? What were your accomplishments while you were President? How long were you President? What did you enjoy most about being President of the United States?

I am President _____

_____

_____

_____

_____

_____

_____

_____

_____

_____

_____

_____

_____

_____

_____

_____

_____

_____

_____

_____

_____

_____

_____

_____

_____

_____

_____

_____

Alliteration Activity

You can write fun poems using words that begin with the same sound. This is called *alliteration*. Pick your favorite state and write a four-line alliterative poem. Look at the examples to help you.

Alaska	Maine
Antarctic Animals	Majestic Mountains
Acrobats in Anchorage	Many Marvelous Marinas
Animate, Alert, and Appealing	Memorable Midday Menus

_____

_____

_____

_____

_____

_____

_____

_____

TWIN 406 - States and Capitals

My Favorite Holiday

Every country has holidays or special celebrations.
Think of your favorite holiday and write a holiday poem.

Line 1:   Name your favorite holiday.
Line 2:   Name two colors you see on this holiday.
Line 3:   Name three kinds of food you eat on this holiday.
Line 4:   Name something you do on this holiday.
Line 5:   Name the month that this holiday occurs.

Christmas
Red and Green
Ham, Turkey, Cookies
Sing Christmas Carols
December

_____

_____

_____

_____

_____

_____

Let's State The Facts

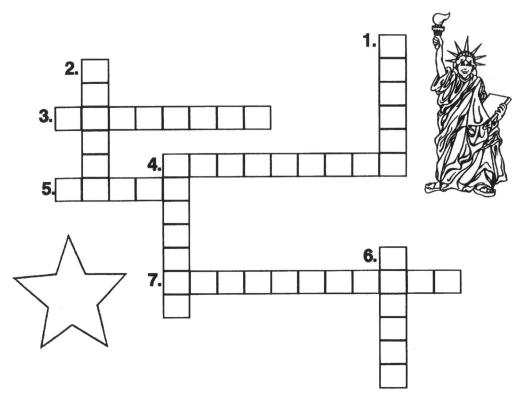

Down

1. The capital of South Dakota
2. The capital of Montana
4. Where you can see the Statue of Liberty
6. Made up of over 130 islands

Across

3. Where Abraham Lincoln was a lawyer
4. The capital of Tennessee
5. Known for its lobsters
7. The smallest state

TWIN 406 - States and Capitals

Find Each State's Bird

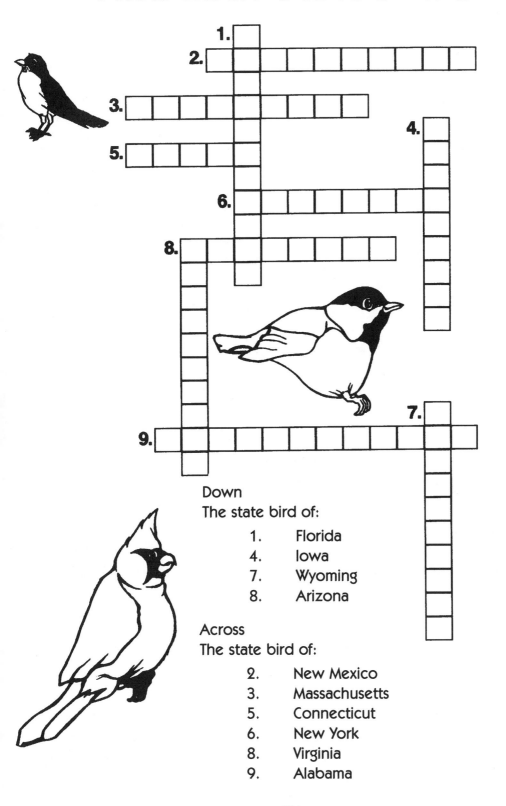

Down
The state bird of:

1. Florida
4. Iowa
7. Wyoming
8. Arizona

Across
The state bird of:

2. New Mexico
3. Massachusetts
5. Connecticut
6. New York
8. Virginia
9. Alabama

TWIN 406 - States and Capitals

Stating Our Capitals

Circle each state's capital in the puzzle. Write the correct capital on the line.

J	A	C	K	S	O	N	I	T	H	P	B	T	T	U
X	U	C	H	E	Y	E	N	N	E	Z	I	P	L	K
L	I	N	C	O	L	N	E	Y	L	Q	S	A	S	M
A	W	D	E	N	V	E	R	R	E	B	M	L	U	O
T	Z	S	S	A	L	E	M	A	N	O	A	N	T	C
U	M	C	O	L	U	M	B	I	A	I	R	I	T	Y
S	T	P	A	U	L	P	O	V	Y	S	C	N	G	L
T	A	L	L	A	H	A	S	S	E	E	K	H	D	S
P	O	L	O	S	H	Y	T	B	O	K	M	K	B	V
C	H	A	R	L	E	S	T	O	N	I	A	R	T	M

Capitals

Columbia	Charleston	Juneau
Lincoln	St. Paul	Denver
Bismarck	Jackson	Tallahassee
Salem	Helena	Boise
	Cheyenne	

1. Wyoming _____
2. North Dakota _____
3. Montana_____
4. Colorado_____
5. Idaho_____
6. Minnesota_____
7. Oregon_____
8. Nebraska_____
9. Florida _____
10. South Carolina _____
11. Mississippi_____
12. Alaska _____
13. West Virginia _____

TWIN 406 - States and Capitals

Stating Our Capitals

Circle each state's capital in the puzzle. Write the correct capital on the line.

A	U	G	U	S	T	A	M	P	N	U	D	T	T	U
U	P	I	E	R	R	E	L	Q	L	M	O	R	T	K
S	C	O	N	C	O	R	D	B	Y	A	V	A	S	M
T	R	I	C	H	M	O	N	D	A	O	E	L	U	O
I	S	N	O	A	B	O	S	T	O	N	R	N	T	C
N	C	A	R	S	O	N	C	I	T	Y	Y	I	T	Y
S	A	N	T	A	F	E	L	A	N	S	I	N	G	L
T	O	P	E	K	A	T	O	P	E	R	I	H	D	S
C	R	C	O	R	P	E	O	L	I	S	K	K	B	V
D	P	I	E	B	R	A	A	D	I	S	N	A	R	T

Capitals

Augusta	Boston	Topeka
Pierre	Concord	Dover
Austin	Carson City	Santa Fe
Albany	Richmond	Lansing

1. Delaware _____
2. Kansas_____
3. Maine_____
4. New York _____
5. Virginia_____
6. Michigan_____

7. New Hampshire_____
8. South Dakota_____
9. Massachusetts_____
10. Texas_____
11. New Mexico _____
12. Nevada _____

Stating Our Capitals

Circle each state's capital in the puzzle. Write the correct capital on the line

S	A	L	T	L	A	K	E	C	I	T	Y	T	T	L
O	K	L	A	H	O	M	A	C	I	T	Y	R	T	I
L	P	H	O	E	N	I	X	S	I	R	R	A	S	T
Y	T	N	A	S	H	V	I	L	L	E	T	L	U	T
M	X	C	O	L	U	M	B	U	S	N	V	E	T	L
P	W	P	L	Q	T	T	F	E	B	T	M	I	P	E
I	A	U	E	T	M	A	D	I	S	O	N	G	O	R
A	N	N	A	P	O	L	I	S	Y	N	K	H	D	O
I	N	D	I	A	N	A	P	O	L	I	S	R	B	C
R	A	P	I	P	M	A	D	I	S	A	N	R	T	K

Capitals

Olympia	Trenton	Phoenix
Columbus	Raleigh	Little Rock
Madison	Oklahoma City	Indianapolis
Salt Lake City	Nashville	Annapolis

1. Wisconsin_____

2. Utah_____

3. Arizona_____

4. Indiana_____

5. Tennessee_____

6. Arkansas_____

7. Washington_____

8. Oklahoma_____

9. New Jersey_____

10. North Carolina_____

11. Maryland_____

12. Ohio_____

TWIN 406 - States and Capitals

Stating Our Capitals

Circle each state's capital in the puzzle. Write the correct capital on the line.

U	J	E	F	F	E	R	S	O	N	C	I	T	Y	D
K	M	O	N	T	G	O	M	E	R	Y	M	D	R	E
T	H	A	R	T	F	O	R	D	E	A	D	Q	S	S
A	E	T	H	O	N	O	L	U	L	U	B	Z	U	M
B	Q	L	M	O	N	T	P	E	L	I	E	R	T	O
A	H	A	R	R	I	S	B	U	R	G	W	X	F	I
T	V	N	P	R	O	V	I	D	E	N	C	E	O	N
O	W	T	S	P	R	I	N	G	F	I	E	L	D	E
N	S	A	C	R	A	M	E	N	T	O	C	N	B	S
R	O	U	G	E	F	R	A	N	K	F	O	R	T	M
A	T	L	A	N	T	A	K	I	D	K	N	S	L	K

Capitals

Montgomery   Baton Rouge   Honolulu
Sacramento   Jefferson City   Springfield
Hartford   Harrisburg   Des Moines
Atlanta   Providence   Frankfort
         Montpelier

1. Vermont _____
2. Rhode Island _____
3. Pennsylvania _____
4. Missouri _____
5. Louisiana _____
6. Alabama _____

7. California _____
8. Georgia _____
9. Hawaii _____
10. Connecticut _____
11. Illinois _____
12. Kentucky _____
13. Iowa _____

15

Facts About The U.S.A.

"From every mountain side, let freedom ring!"
"I pledge allegiance to the flag of the United States of America
and to the republic for which it stands: one nation under God,
indivisible, with liberty and justice for all."

I am proud to be a citizen in a nation where I am free.
The United States of America is a country of liberty.
"In God we trust," we do believe. We recite our pledge with pride.
The fifty states are all unique; it doesn't matter where you reside.
From California to eastern Maine, we'll visit every state.
We're a melting pot of different folks; I think we're all first rate.

I want to learn about my country and learn about each state.
I want to learn all the facts that make our nation great!
I want to visit all the states in the U.S.A.
and sing their names each and every day!

Let's learn them in order...alphabetically's the way
we're going to teach you the states of the U.S. of A.
Now listen to the facts. There are quite a few,
so we'll sing a song as a little review.

The camellia is its flower with dark green leaves;
Alabama is the state with the warm summer breeze.
Beautiful **Alaska**, our last frontier state—
the Eskimos will tell you it's the dog sledding place.
Now in sunny **Arizona**, the climate's hot and dry.
The wondrous Grand Canyon will surely catch your eye.
The "Land of Opportunity," the mockingbird's coo,
are all a part of **Arkansas'** countryside too.
Go west to **California**. See the San Diego Zoo,
or Disneyland, Hollywood, the ocean deep and blue.
In **Colorado**, mountains are covered with snow,
making skiing quite appealing, so off we go!
The state of **Connecticut**, it's eastward bound...
where the American Robin can often be found.
Delaware was first to approve the U.S. Constitution,
and fight the British in the American Revolution.
In the state of **Florida** let's take a flight—yeah,
to Cape Canaveral's chief launching site.
An end to slavery the Civil War brought
in the state of **Georgia** where cotton was sought.
(**Chorus**)

Tropical **Hawaii**, in 1959, became our 50th state.
There the sun will always shine.
In **Idaho** there's farming, potatoes, wheat, and sheep.
Or travel down Snake River, which is really unique.
Lincoln was a lawyer in the state of **Illinois**.
He studied very hard when he was a young boy.
In **Indiana**, you can watch a famous auto race called the Indy 500.
Better keep up with the pace.
The state of **Iowa** has rich and fertile soil,
for corn and soybeans make all the farmers toil.
Laura Ingalls Wilder wrote books about the plains.
In the state of **Kansas**, her cabin still remains.
Kentucky is often called the "Bluegrass State".
Watch the thoroughbred horses race out of the gate.
Louisiana's known for all of their parades
when the Mardi Gras festival comes their way.
In **Maine**, you'll find crabs and lobsters galore;
all kinds of seafood can be caught off their shore.
In **Maryland** a man named Francis Scott Key wrote
the Star Spangled Banner—"Oh say, can you see?"
(**Chorus**)

The state of **Massachusetts** was the home of Paul Revere,
who warned us that the American Revolution was near.

Michigan's the place that gave Henry Ford his start.
In Detroit, that's where they make a lot of car parts.
The tree of **Minnesota** is the Red Norway Pine,
and visit the "Twin Cities" where you'll have a good time.
In **Mississippi** you can take a steamboat ride.
Watch the paddle wheel turn as the shore goes by.
Climb the Ozark Mountains in the "Show Me State."
In **Missouri**, the St. Louis Arch is just great!
In **Montana**, the Rockies are topped with snow.
The Yellowstone River can be seen below.
Nebraska's the place for raising cattle.
The weather, of course, the farmers must battle.
The dry sunny climate in **Nevada's** desert towns
encourages vacationers all year round.
New Hampshire's scenic beauty will make you sigh,
as the many green forests gently landscape the sky.
New Jersey is found on our eastern shore.
There's the Atlantic City Boardwalk and so much more.
(**Chorus**)

View the Rio Grande River on a sunny day.
New Mexico's the place where I want to stay.
The Statue of Liberty is quite a view.
In the state of **New York**, there's Niagara Falls, too.
In **North Carolina** the first airplane flight was conducted
by the Wright brothers. Oh, what a sight!
In **North Dakota**, where the great plains lie,
where the Sioux Indian tribe roamed in days gone by.
In **Ohio** there's the Pro Football Hall of Fame.
In the "Buckeye State," it's a popular game!
Oklahoma is known for the wild rodeo.
There the cowboys put on a real western show.
In the state of **Oregon**, that's where they made their mark,
the great expedition of Lewis and Clark.
Pennsylvania is the state in which General Lee fought
the Battle of Gettysburg in 1863.
Did you know **Rhode Island** is our smallest state—
Less than 50 miles wide at its broadest place?
Now, **South Carolina**, it's simply grand.
Let's visit the beach and play in the sand.
(**Chorus**)

Four presidents' faces are forever carved in stone.
In **South Dakota**, Mt. Rushmore is well-known.
The Grand Ole Opry can be found in Nashville, **Tennessee**.
The Country Music Hall of Fame is there for all to see.
Let's visit the Alamo where brave soldiers fought.
Independence in **Texas** is what they sought.
The climate is dry, the land forms are rare.
In **Utah**, the alcoves will make you stare.
The Appalachian Trail in **Vermont**, you'll find,
offers cross-country skiing—those trails sure wind.
Hey **Virginia**! We would like to give you a hand,
for Washington and Jefferson lived on your land.
Washington state can be found on the Pacific.
The Cascade Range—its view is just terrific.
The Appalachian Mountains you are going to find
in the state of **West Virginia**, where they also mine.
The state of **Wisconsin** is famous for its lakes,
and all of the milk and cheese that it makes.
Many wild animals still make their home out in
Wyoming where they are free to roam.
(**Chorus**)

16

Singing Our States

Al - a - bam - a and A - lask - a, Ar - i - zo - na, Ar - kan - sas, Cal - i -

for - nia, Col - o - ra - do, I like this, Ma! Conn - ec - ti - cut and Del - a - ware, then Flo - ri - da is next. But—

Geor - gia and Ha - wai - i real - ly are best. I - da - ho,— Ill - in - ois,—

In - di - an - a, I - o - wa,— Kan - sas and Ken - tuck - y, Lou - i - si - an - a, Maine,

Mar - y - land and Mass - a - chu - setts, Mich - i - gan, YAY! Min - ne -

so - ta, Mis - sis - sip - pi, Mis - sou - ri and more, there's Mon - tan - a and Ne - bra - ska, I like this score. Ne -

va - da and New Hamp - shire, New Jer - sey's real - ly neat. New— Mex - i - co and New— York just can't be beat! North

17

Car - o - li - na, North Da - ko - ta, O - hi - o___ and O - kla - ho - ma,

Or - e - gon, there's Penn - syl - van - ia and Rhode Is - land, too. South Car - o - li - na, South Da - ko - ta, YA HOO!

Well, there's Ten - nes - see and Tex - as, then there's U - tah, I say,

Ver - mont and Vir - gin - ia, now you've made my day. Wash - ing - ton and West Vir - gin - ia and Wis - con - sin my friend, and Wy -

om - ing is the last state and we've made it to the end! We have learned the fif - ty states

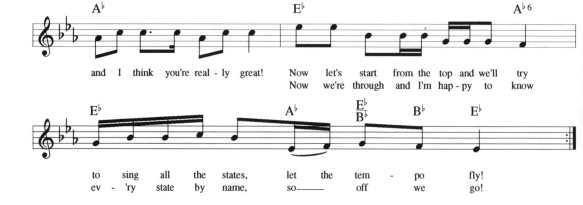

and   I   think   you're   real - ly   great!   Now   let's   start   from   the   top   and   we'll   try
Now   we're   through   and   I'm   hap - py   to   know

to   sing   all   the   states,   let   the   tem - po   fly!
ev - 'ry   state   by   name,   so___   off   we   go!

Learning Our Capitals

Mont - gom - 'ry. Al - a - bam - a, Ju - neau, Al - ask - a,

Phoen - ix, Ar - i - zo - na and Lit - tle Rock, — Ar - kan - sas. Sac - ra - men - to, Cal - i - for - nia,

Den - ver, Col - o - ra - do, Hart - ford, Con - nect - i - cut and Do - ver, Del - a - ware.

Tal - la - has - see, Flor - i - da, At - lan - ta, Geor - gia, Hon - o - lu - lu, Ha - wai - i, —

Boi - se, — I - da - ho. Spring - field, — Ill - i - nois, In - dian - ap - 'lis, In - di - an - a,

Des - Moines, — I - o - wa, — Frank - fort, Ken - tuck - y! To - pek - a, Kan - sas,

Bat - on Rouge, Lou - i - si - an - a, Aug - us - ta, Maine —— and Ann - ap - 'lis, Mar - y - land!

TWIN 406 - States and Capitals

Bos - ton, Mass - a - chu - setts,— Lans - ing, Mich - i - gan,— Saint Paul, Min - ne - so - ta,

Jack - son, Mis - sis - sip - pi. Jef - fer - son Cit - y, Mis - sour - i, Hel - en - a, Mon - tan - a,

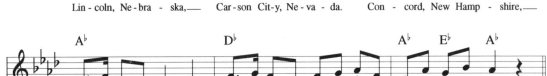

Lin - coln, Ne - bra - ska,— Car - son Cit - y, Ne - va - da. Con - cord, New Hamp - shire,—

Tren - ton, New Jer - sey, San - ta Fe, New Mex - i - co,— Al - ban - y, New York.

Ral - eigh, North Car - o - lin - a, Bismarck, North Da - ko - ta, Col - um - bus, O - hi - o, Ok - la -

ho - ma Cit - y, Ok - la - ho - ma, Sa - lem,— Or - e - gon,— Har - ris - burg, Penn - syl - va - nia,

Prov - i - dence, Rhode Is - land, Co - lum - bia, South Car - o - lin - a. Pier - re, South Da - ko - ta,

Nash - ville, Ten - ne - see,—— Aus - tin,— Tex - as,— Salt Lake Cit - y, U - tah,

20

Mont - pe - li - er, Ver - mont,— Rich - mond, Vir - gin - ia, O - lym - pia, Wash - ing - ton,—

Charles - ton, West Vir - gin - ia. Mad - i - son, Wis - con - sin,— Chey - enne, Wy - om - ing.

These are the last two states, A - mer - i - ca, you're great!

"America! America! God shed His grace on thee,
and crown thy good with brotherhood, from sea to shining sea!"

It's your turn now, sing aloud. Sit up straight, and be proud.
I'll say the capital; you say the state.
Listen to the music—don't be late! C'mon...

Montgomery...	Topeka...	Bismarck...
Juneau...	Baton Rouge...	Columbus...
Phoenix...	Augusta...	Oklahoma City...
and Little Rock...	Annapolis...	Salem...
Sacramento...	Boston...	Harrisburg...
Denver...	Lansing...	Providence...
Hartford...	St. Paul...	Columbia...
and Dover...	and Jackson...	Pierre...
Tallahassee...	Jefferson City...	Nashville...
Atlanta...	Helena...	Austin...
Honolulu...	Lincoln...	Salt Lake City...
Boise...	Carson City...	Montpelier...
Springfield...	Concord...	Richmond...
Indianapolis...	Trenton...	Olympia...
Des Moines...	Santa Fe...	and Charleston...
and Frankfort...	Albany...	Madison...
	Raleigh...	Cheyenne...

We've learned the capitals of all the states.
Wow, you sure are great!
I'm proud to live in America, the land of liberty,
where there are 50 states in the U.S.A.
We're learning all our capitals today.
I know every one of the 50 states in this land of liberty!

States & Capitals Study Guide

Name	Capital	Abbreviation
Alabama	Montgomery	AL
Alaska	Juneau	AK
Arizona	Phoenix	AZ
Arkansas	Little Rock	AR
California	Sacramento	CA
Colorado	Denver	CO
Connecticut	Hartford	CT
Delaware	Dover	DE
Florida	Tallahassee	FL
Georgia	Atlanta	GA
Hawaii	Honolulu	HI
Idaho	Boise	ID
Illinois	Springfield	IL
Indiana	Indianapolis	IN
Iowa	Des Moines	IA
Kansas	Topeka	KS
Kentucky	Frankfort	KY
Louisiana	Baton Rouge	LA
Maine	Augusta	ME
Maryland	Annapolis	MD
Massachusetts	Boston	MA
Michigan	Lansing	MI
Minnesota	St. Paul	MN
Mississippi	Jackson	MS
Missouri	Jefferson City	MO

Name	Capital	Abbreviation
Montana	Helena	MT
Nebraska	Lincoln	NE
Nevada	Carson City	NV
New Hampshire	Concord	NH
New Jersey	Trenton	NJ
New Mexico	Santa Fe	NM
New York	Albany	NY
North Carolina	Raleigh	NC
North Dakota	Bismarck	ND
Ohio	Columbus	OH
Oklahoma	Oklahoma City	OK
Oregon	Salem	OR
Pennsylvania	Harrisburg	PA
Rhode Island	Providence	RI
South Carolina	Columbia	SC
South Dakota	Pierre	SD
Tennessee	Nashville	TN
Texas	Austin	TX
Utah	Salt Lake City	UT
Vermont	Montpelier	VT
Virginia	Richmond	VA
Washington	Olympia	WA
West Virginia	Charleston	WV
Wisconsin	Madison	WI
Wyoming	Cheyenne	WY

Our Fifty States

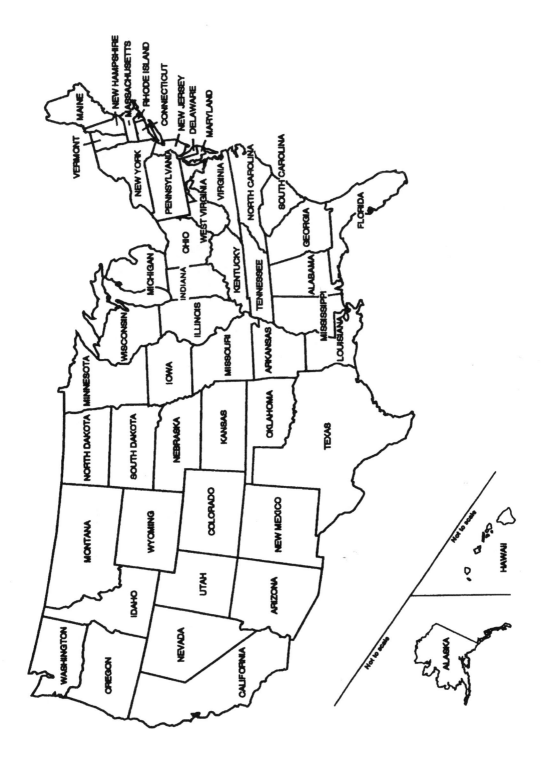

WASHINGTON
OREGON
CALIFORNIA
NEVADA
IDAHO
UTAH
ARIZONA
MONTANA
WYOMING
COLORADO
NEW MEXICO
NORTH DAKOTA
SOUTH DAKOTA
NEBRASKA
KANSAS
OKLAHOMA
TEXAS
MINNESOTA
IOWA
MISSOURI
ARKANSAS
LOUISIANA
WISCONSIN
ILLINOIS
MICHIGAN
INDIANA
OHIO
KENTUCKY
TENNESSEE
MISSISSIPPI
ALABAMA
GEORGIA
FLORIDA
SOUTH CAROLINA
NORTH CAROLINA
VIRGINIA
WEST VIRGINIA
PENNSYLVANIA
NEW YORK
VERMONT
MAINE
NEW HAMPSHIRE
MASSACHUSETTS
RHODE ISLAND
CONNECTICUT
NEW JERSEY
DELAWARE
MARYLAND
HAWAII
ALASKA

Not to scale

©Twin Sisters Productions, Inc.

TWIN 406 - States and Capitals

Page 10

Crossword answers:

1. PIERRE
2. HELEN
3. ILLINOIS
4. NASHVILLE
5. MAINE
6. HAWAII
7. RHODE ISLAND

(Down: NEW YORK)

Page 11

1. MCCIKING
2. ROADRUNNER
3. CHICKADEE
4. GOLDFINCH
5. ROBIN
6. BLUEBIRD
7. MEADOWLARK
8. CARDINAL
9. YELLOWHAMMER

(Down: CACTUSWREN)

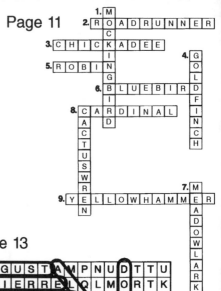

Page 12

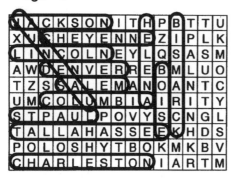

Word search:

JACKSON ITHPBTTU
XU CHEYENNE ZIPLK
LINCOLN EYLQSASM
AW DENVER REBMLUO
TZS SALEM ANOANTC
UMCOLUMBIA IRITY
STPAUL POVYSCNGL
TALLAHASSEE KHDS
POLOSHYTBOKMKBV
CHARLESTON IARTM

Wyoming–Cheyenne
North Dakota–Bismarck
Montana–Helena
Colorado–Denver
Idaho–Boise
Minnesota–St. Paul

Oregon–Salem
Nebraska–Lincoln
Florida–Tallahassee
South Carolina–Columbia
Mississippi–Jackson
Alaska–Juneau
West Virginia–Charleston

Page 13

Word search:

AUGUSTA MPNUDTTU
UPIERRE OLMORTK
SCONCORD BYAVASM
TRICHMOND AOELUO
ISNO ABOSTON RNTC
NCARSON CITY YITY
SANTA FE LANSING L
TOPEKA TOPERIHDS
CRCORPEOLISKKBV
OPIEBRAADISNART

Delaware–Dover
Kansas–Topeka
Maine–Augusta
New York–Albany
Virginia–Richmond
Michigan–Lansing

New Hampshire–Conco
South Dakota–Pierre
Massachusetts–Boston
Texas–Austin
New Mexico–Santa Fe
Nevada–Carson City

Page 14

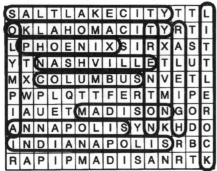

Word search:

SALTLAKECITY TTL
OKLAHOMACITY RTI
LPHOENIX SIRXAST
YTNASHVILLE TLUT
MXCOLUMBUSNVETL
PWPLQTTFERTMIPE
IAUET MADISON GOR
ANNAPOLIS YNKHDO
INDIANAPOLIS RBC
RAPIPMADISANRTK

Wisconsin–Madison
Utah–Salt Lake City
Arizona–Phoenix
Indiana–Indianapolis
Tennessee–Nashville
Arkansas–Little Rock

Washington–Olympia
Oklahoma–Oklahoma City
New Jersey–Trenton
North Carolina–Raleigh
Maryland–Annapolis
Ohio–Columbus

Page 15

Word search:

UJEFFERSONCITY D
KMONTGOMERY MDRE
THARTFORD EADQSS
AETHONOLULU BZUM
BQLMONTPELIER TO
AHARRISBURG WXPI
TVNPROVIDENCE ON
OWTSPRINGFIELDE
NSACRAMENTOCNBS
ROUGE FRANKFORT M
ATLANTA KIDKNSLK

Vermont–Montpelier
Rhode Island–Providence
Pennsylvania–Harrisburg
Missouri–Jefferson City
Louisiana–Baton Rouge
Alabama–Montgomery

California–Sacramento
Georgia–Atlanta
Hawaii–Honolulu
Connecticut–Hartford
Illinois–Springfield
Kentucky–Frankfort
Iowa–Des Moines

TWIN 406 - States and Capital

8263013